LIBERATED WOMAN

A BLACK GIRL'S JOURNEY TO SELF LOVE

VOLUME 1

BETRICE COLEMAN-SWEET

Print ISBN: 978-1-098-38510-1
eBook ISBN: 978-1-098-38511-8

Dedicated to the realest story I ever wrote, My Ray of Light.
For the babies with babies whose richness is unbeknownst to them. I hear
you, I see you, I LOVE YOU!

IN THE BEGINNING

(1987-2003)

LIBERATED WOMAN

I am a liberated woman, you see.

I may be a girl to you, but I am a woman to me.

Some people say, "Child, don't go so fast, you still have time. If you were a real woman you would be trying to make a dime."

I don't need a job and my time is running out.

Some people call me delirious and others call me a snout.

My definition of a woman is a person who has her own ways.

The age starts at twelve and runs until you're old and gray.

One day, a woman asked me "Does your mother know about you, being a woman as you say around this here town?"

So when I told my mother, she slapped me down!

She said, "Girl don't go so fast! I still want you to make your dreams come true. Be smart and don't be a fool. And if you don't stop this woman thing, I will be at your throat!" And then she said

"All I am trying to say

Is don't try to live your life in one day

So when my mother told me what I was doing was a mistake

I decided to be real instead of fake

So I will leave my pretend life with a smile.

Instead of trying to be a woman, I will enjoy being a child.

NOW AND THEN

Now, Black people are struggling for equal rights and are free
We are bright and we are filled with integrity.
We fight for our rights and we are brave
But some people remember when Blacks were slaves
We are victims of enslavement, you see
Blacks cared for each other; yes we were and still are a minority
We were treated like animals, beaten and even killed.
We starved with dirty clothes, yet even still
We looked up at the morning sun
With our terrible life and hoped for a better one
To earn all of our rights
We had to struggle and fight
An example put by the Rev. Dr. Martin Luther King
He is the one who helped us to let freedom ring
He is known to us with honor and fame
His legacy still burns like an everlasting flame
We cried, we sighed, we hoped and protested
We even bowed our heads and we got down on our knees.
Because we wanted all inequality to cease
So I hope that day come soon for all equality
So there will be a better world for you and for me.
So when hard times come your way
Don't just sit there and bow
Think of all the struggling we had to do in the past
And how you can achieve your dream now
So just think this in your head

Of all the victories and triumphs we've led

I know who I am and I am proud of who I am and I'm going to let people know out loud

That I am Black and I am Proud.

No one can judge me by my way of living or my face

No one can judge me by my race

They have to judge for what is in the inside, not the outside

We take great joy and pride

We even had a whole month set aside

For all the heroes and heroines who set us on track

Because they wanted everyone in every city, and every state

To know how it feels and what it means to be black

Life may be hard, as though it may seem

You have to use all your ability

To achieve your dream

Because those people paved the way

They want us to see equality someday.

CODE OF PEACE

We the people
Should respect each other
We are all brothers and sisters
Do not discriminate
It only causes hate
Don't let your eyes manipulate
Your mind
What you see is not what you may find
Be the best you can be
Always Remember LOVE is the key

CONFESSIONS OF A SPECIAL GIRL

He said don't tell
Because what we did was bad
I could not scream or yell
I just held it in with all I had
At 4 years old
All I could recall
Was to do what I was told
A child should be seen and not heard at all
The things that I was told to do
Was because he said I was a "Special" girl
I wonder if at the time anyone knew
Or was I the only one caught in this destructive world
The years passed and I
Still nothing was seen
It became such a part of my life
That everything was routine
I would dread for my parents or any adults to leave
As time went on
It was hard for me to believe
What was going on was hard for me to conceive
So I began to feel "Special"
And that this was love at its best
Disturbed, confused, abused, and violated
Each day I grew from a girl to a young woman I hated
Yet, He said I was "Special"
At the time I felt he was the only one

No one else thought it was crucial

On how life changed drastically since it has begun

No one told me about how "Special" my first time should be

No one sat down and had that "Special" talk about the birds and the bees

No one came to my defense

Even in my rage of acting out, It did not make sense

At the age of 12, I spoke of these events

But no one listened

I was proven guilty instead of innocent

A million showers couldn't wash away the dirt

Maybe a hug and some consoling could have eased the hurt

Still yet I was "Special"

I cried louder

Yet the "Special" girl still went unheard

All my accusations they say were absurd

So I decided to silence myself

Thoughts of death and great pain is what I felt

I became "Special" to the abusers and users

And the ones who say they care about my well being

However, could not take the time to see what I was seeing

The Innocence Lost for a Special Girl

SHINE

Shine the light
Shine it bright
So we all can see at night
Let it free
Whatever it may be
So we all can see
Don't be blue
If you are true
And what the best can do for you
Let it out
Let it shout
To see what life is all about
Warm the cold
In your soul
Before you grow old
In your heart
In your mind
Let it start
Let it shine

YOUNG LOVE

Love is tender
Love is strong
Sometimes harmful
Sometimes wrong
Your heart is filled with glee
Without Love,
It's sad, you see
So believe in your love and they will believe in you
I hope the love you have together can always remain true
I love you with all my heart
I've felt that way from the start
You'll hold my hand and squeeze it tight
Together we stand all through the night
The hugs and kisses are like a dream
But don't squeeze too tight or you'll make me scream
Me with you and you with me
But I think it is time to come to reality.

WHAT YOU ARE

You are the one that can't compete
Because you are so kind and sweet
You are the one that I think of at night
I really like your style
I really like your smile
I wish you could see
That I can hold you close to me
I would never hurt you
Or get mad at the silly things you do
I would never be mad or never cry
Because your my sweet lullaby
Think you are so kind and never mean
Because you are the cutest girl that I ever seen
You are the one that makes my head spin you see
Because I really like you and I hope you like me
You are the one that is so true
I want you to know
I love you.

A HEART IS FRAGILE

A heart is fragile
Delicate like a blooming flower
A heart is clean
Like being washed by an April shower
A heart is soft
Like a big, fluffy, pillow, you see
A heart is not to be handled foolishly
A heart can shine
Like a bright star
A heart pumps and beats
Wherever you are
A heart is fragile like a glass
When it falls it can be broke in half
A heart is sensitive and gentle within
It will beat according to your feelings until the end
Sweet, kind, hard, stubborn, and smart
All of these things and more describes these feelings and ways of
a heart

SUMMER RAIN

When the air is dry
When there is a sign of pain
When you hear a loud cry
It is time for summer rain
The rain pours down
Like a waterfall
The streets will drown
It won't hesitate at all
The air will feel hot
The ground feels wet
As the sun set
The grass continues to grow
The trees continue to stand
Because they already know
The rain gives them a helping hand
And its hard for us to understand
 Mother nature is beautiful
And it is clear to see
That she wants to keep the world full
And wants all things in the world to be free.

THE NIGHT HAS A MILLION EYES

The night has a million eyes
For I have only two
There is where the beauty lies
They shine right through
They sparkle and twinkle
So we can see their glow
Their warmth and structure
They gladly show
The night has a million eyes
To see a million dreams
In which everyone hold inside
They are well hidden and not to be seen
When they wake up
Love fills the air
And lots of other wonderful stuff
You can tell when the feeling is there
The eyes can see everyone
And everything you do
At night
They can tell how you are feeling to
They warm your heart
With every sight
Because they are the million eyes of the night.

BACK IN TIME

Back in time when we were mistreated
Because of the color of our skin
When Blacks couldn't come out with their feelings
So they kept it within
When the black minority were used as slaves
But we still thought about hope, and we were brave
With all the beatings, hurt and sorrow
We still hoped for a better tomorrow
We still held our heads up high
Praying to God Almighty in the sky
So we came together with our goals and love
Hoping courage would come from the Heavens above
We protested and struggled with all our might
Oh yes, we put up a great and powerful fight
With all the heroes and heroines that set us on track
Which made each moment exciting, you see.
In every step of the way
It lead us to victory.
Freedom and justice for blacks and for all.
Which made us braver than ever and we stood tall
So I would like to thank them for all they have done
For all the courage and victories won.
I also would like to thank the One above
Who filled our hearts with joy and love
Furthermore, I would like to say
If it was not for these important people

I wouldn't be standing here today

It just shows that everybody can become

Somebody in this here crowd.

Because I am black and I'm proud.

Blacks made it from the bottom to the top with intelligence as
a sign

If it wasn't for the people back in time.

HE IS WITHIN YOU

Whenever you are sad
Whenever you are blue
Whenever you are mad
Call on God because he is within you
Whenever you need help
And you don't know what to do
Just look within yourself
And ask God because he is within you
Whenever you have sinned and think nobody knew
Well think again because God knows too
Remember, when you thought you had a lot of friends
But only had a few
Remember when you couldn't make your problems end
The answers are within
God is the best friend that you could talk to
Remember when you won something by accident
And you did not have a clue
Where it comes from
Just remember God is within you.

QUEEN OF GOSPEL: AN ODE TO MAHALIA JACKSON

Who I am
Is who I'll be
Because I have great dignity
I was born to sing
And hear bells ring
When I was small
My Mama knew nothing at all
Of how my voice was high and tall
Then everyone began to notice my voice
Without a trace and without a choice
Little girl with a big voice
Is what people called me
Then I was heard around every state and every city
In my city, people listen to the blues
They wear fancy clothes and fancy shoes
Such people as. Bessie Smith and Lady Day
In all blues they say
How down they were feeling, you see
When I sing, I want people to shout for joy and be happy
Us Black people couldn't go on the white people's territory
Because they thought we are full of ignorance and stupidity
But God made us different from each other
We have a different father and a different mother
That's why I chose to sing Gospel, you see
To show my love and dignity

I sing Gospel for you and for me

Because us Black People are intelligent and courageous, you see

When I died

I didn't want you to sigh or cry

Because I will be in a place in the sky

I'll be in a place where there's freedom and justice, you see

I'll be in a place with no hatred or misery

If you want to know more about me

Ask someone in your family

And then if they don't have much to tell

Then remember me as Mahalia Jackson

The Queen of Gospel

CONGRATULATIONS RENITA

Congratulations to a person who is so dear

You come so far and now you are really here

You did your best and stayed on the right track

You didn't have any doubts

And you didn't step back

You kept on stepping forward

And you reached a high step

With lots of love, lots of support, lots of help

You stood proud and tall

So everyone would see

That hard work and studying

Pays of beautifully

You faced a lot of hardship and had many problems

You had friendships which helped you solve them

To a person who is wise and very bold

May you continue to accomplish your dreams and your goals

May God bless you and may you be the best in everything that
you do

Congratulations Renita

We love you!

IN A WORLD ALL ALONE

No one understands me
Not knowing how I feel
Pushing me away like a dummy
Not knowing that I am real
I never could express
How I feel inside
Instead I get depressed
And let my feelings hide
When you try to show
Just how much you care
They take advantage of you
And act like you wasn't there
The only thing I ask
Which is so easy to do
Is for someone to look me straight in the eye
And say, "I love you too"
I don't know what's wrong
Or what's happening
Or what's going on
Or is it just me
So would someone please let me know
So I could feel at ease
So everyone can know my feelings
I would like to know the answer please
Maybe I should be stubborn and selfish
Like some people I know are

But I'll continue to be myself
Until I go far
I'm still feeing low
Still feeling blue
To those people who uses attitude and take advantage of me
I love you too.

LIFE IS LIKE

Life is like a dream
In which, you are running against time
Life is like a shell
Which in it there is something great to find
Life is like a story
That has not been told
Your heart is a house
Which cannot be sold
It may surprise you
Make you rich and famous
Or cut you like a knife
That's what's in store with iife

WEEKENDS

Weekends are fun
Weekends are times for play
Out in the sun
We play all day
It is a time to be free
From all the hard work and pain
To be happy
And sing in the rain
It is a time to go to the mall
And talk on the phone
A time to be tall
And not be alone
It is time to relax and take a rest
Forget about the facts
And don't settle for less
It is a time to put all things aside
When all problems end
No one can hide the fun of a weekend

ALCOHOLISM

It brings you down
It makes you crazy
You may feel like your going to drown
And your head gets hazy
It soothes the pain
For a little while
But then the dreariness begins to gain
And easiness runs out of style
Your thoughts are not in gear
And sometimes you lose yourself
Then you wish that your senses were here
And you may hurt someone else
So what's the purpose of going through all of this dismay
When your mind can have a surface
And you can face a brighter day
When there are problems
Don't take a fall
Just sit there and try to solve them
Instead of turning to alcohol

SWEET LOVE

What is love

That is what the question is about

What do you think of?

When you hear the word out

Is it pure?

Is it sweet?

Is it sure?

That it is hard to meet

I held your hand

And you held mine

Together we stand

As we face time

I don't know what it is

That makes me feel this way

All I know is whatever it is

Makes me think about you everyday

I don't know how you feel

I hope the same

I hope this is real

And you are not playing a game

If it is love

Then I love you very much

Because you are so sweet as a dove

And I quiver with your every touch

It may be harmful

It may be nice

But right now it is wonderful
And I will make that sacrifice
So what I want to know
From you and the one above
How far will we go
And what is love?

UNTITLED

The hardships of life can take a toll
No matter how dumb or smart or young or old
It brings you down so very low
That you feel like there is no escape
No place to go
Yeah, life's obstacles ain't no kind of joy
It feels as everything around you fall apart and destroy
Well, Life's problems.
Need I say more
And at each new one seems more difficult
Than the one before
It sometimes may not be that big at all
All just tests to see how you can stand
As a strong individual
Damn, what we wouldn't do without stress
Which goes along the core of all tests
I will make things right
No matter how long it takes
I will stand and fight
In every move that I make
I will make things right
Because it has to be done
Taking all that's precious in sight
And bonding it into one
I will stand strong
There is much I must achieve

You may say it's wrong
But this is what I believe
I will supply love
For it bonds things together
Sent from heaven above
And should last forever
Why be afraid
To love, Do you know how
There may be no time to push it away
Why not experience it now
I will open my eyes
To all I have to see

MY TEARS

Like the sky crying when an angel has fallen

Like the wind blowing

When mother nature is calling

Like the songs of joy

When a baby comes out of the womb

Like rainbows dancing

When Jesus came out of the tomb

Like the sun gracing us with a light that shines

Like to see the children

Grow throughout our time

Like the severe pain

Of a stab or a cut

Like the sight of the blood running out

Because the cut cannot shut

To know that you will never see someone you love again

Or until your time on earth will end

To overcome my anger, my pain, my hurt, happiness, my joy, my love and my fears

There is not anything that could be more soothing, therapeutic and motivating

Than my tears

NEW YEARS RESOLUTION 1993 FOR A 16 TEEN MOM WITH A NEWBORN SON

1. To strive and work hard for my son and myself

2. Always put his needs before mine

3. To act and be a mature mother and woman

4. To believe in myself and my judgement

5. To make this new year a much better one for RaShaun

6. Always be appreciative and never selfish

7. Do well in all my school classes

8. And last but not least and most important, Pray as much as I can for the Lord's guidance as I go through this year

SHE

We met so long ago
Babies going to school
I saw you but didn't want you to know
Cause I didn't want to look like a fool
Now we are grown
And baby, you are still fine
And now I still want
To make you mine
She's beautiful -mind and body
An intriguing form of art
She can mesmerize everybody
And control their hearts
She has this effect on those
Friends
Who are so very close
That makes them do all kinds of things
And with them she
Has had some type of fling
I often sit and wonder
Does all of this attention go to her head
Or does she not want to
Deal with it all instead
I was so deeply in love
She had me under her spell
Did everything I could think of
To make our lives a fairytale

I could see her pain
The pain she tries to disguise
It's all right there
When I look into her eyes
Some say she has stories
Of events that she
Said occurred
Maybe it's because she wants to be heard
I try to tell her day by day
In all that she will do
You must truly be real with yourself
In order for others to honestly be true to you
Even when those whom
Act sheisty on the side
Soon she will see their bullshit
With her own eyes
Why doesn't she listen to me
Why does she push me away
Or is it just my obsession
So I could see her everyday
How I long to please her
And put a smile on her face
How I wish I could lay down with her
And feel her warm embrace
I guess when she is hurt by so many
She doesn't know who to trust
She slowly becomes those whom she despises so much

LYRICS OF THE HEART

My heart sings a song
My heart is never blue
It sings all day long
And the song is about you
The tune is soft and sweet
A smooth melody
Only one thing makes it complete
It's you being with me
My heart sings a song
You'll hear it loud and clear
It sings all day long
Especially when you are near
If you look into my eyes
You could read the words
They are all truth and no lies
Each feeling seen and heard
My heart sings a song
And with each embrace
The rhythm gets strong
But remains to sustain its grace
My song is just a solo
But what if our hearts met
Together our hearts will grow
Making our solos to a duet
Just imagine the beauty
Even if just for a moment in time

For it to truly be
My heart in yours and your heart in mine
No words have to be spoken
Just the look in your eyes
You could see the precious token
All truth and never any lies
So our hearts will sing a song
Our hearts will never be blue
It will sing it all year long
The song is about love
Between me and you

FAKERY

Fakery is alive and well

Do you know how I can tell

Why do you say you're my friend

And stab and hurt me in the end

What did I ever do to you

But have your back and stay true

How could your heart be so cold

You don't even know the great power that you hold

That could be used in such a good way

 But you never have anything good to say

You smile in my face

And try to embrace

Me....Why?

Tell me how you truly feel

You cannot even be real

Cause that fakery consumed your being

You are blind to love, happiness, inner peace

Negative is what you are seeing

Don't you understand

That fakery has its own plan

And if you allow it to win

You will lose over and over again

What you really don't see

 Is that you are surrounded by fakery

You will never have true friends, true love, true happiness for anyone else

Because you do not even have those things for yourself
Whatever happens in your life
All the struggle and strife
You bring it to you
No one else but you
So if fakery is how you survive
From day to day
Then it is sad cause love not survival is the only way
To succeed and achieve
All you must do is believe
And you will see the change
And all the bitter, anger and hurt will rearrange
And then and only then will you truly see
That you do not have to live off of fakery!

REALIZATION

As the years go by and I start to finally get the grasp on life itself.
I realize a couple of essential guidelines

1) Is to always love yourself

2) Give as much love as you can to others without losing
   the love that you have for yourself

3) To understand the words and actions of others, you
   must first understand yourself: Listen to your voice

4) The most important love is the universal language.
   God gave us that special gift. Many do not know or
   even understand that they have it.

5) Many people confuse love for hurt, anger, rage , and
   sorrow
   Love is all around us. Love is within us
   Love does not hurt and hurt does not love

PEACE OF MIND

Need a peace of mind
So I can sit down and think
I don't want to do anything else
Not even breathe or blink
My mind feels so imprisoned
And it needs to be set free
It needs to be reprogrammed and reconditioned
Which will makes it better for me
My mind needs that positive energy
To flow throughout its being
I need the same thing for my body
Together, they will be agreeing
I need a peace of mind
Release the madness and the stress
Replacing them with love
That is the very best
I need a peace of mind
Cause if I go on there is no hope
I cannot do this anymore
I can no longer cope
No one understands
Except for myself
This is my journey to walk
And I cannot leave it to someone else
I need a peace of mind
That is to say the least
Cause now I truly find
That my mind needs to be at peace

TAKE IT BACK

Take it back
Take back the nights
I held you close
The times when we knew that we were doing the most
Take it back
The hurt that I felt for so long
And the way you was doing me was so wrong
Take back the times when you said you loved me
And that you would never hurt me
The promises that you made
The tears that I cried
The sacrifices
The true love
That I really thought was there
That not wanting me
Not needing me
Not loving me
The not touching me
Take it back
Because
It does not matter to you
When it should have
Now my eyes are open
And I see what does matter
What is important
Not me or my love or my heart

Selfish
Am I
Should I have a reason to be
Maybe
Because you won't take it back
You won't let me go
But to your amazement
I am already gone
So do yourself a favor
Before anything else goes further
Take all your bullshit back

HOT SUMMER DAY

It's a hot summer day
The kids are out to play
As I relax, meditate and lay
Everything and everyone
Beautiful in every way
Life is great at this point
I must say
It's hot and humid
Barely feeling any breeze
There are so many few days as these
You know those where
You could put your mind at ease
So simple with happiness
And love
Very pleased
The heat is strong
And the sun is shining bright
No pressure of any rain, sadness, or troubles in sight
And you know everything is going to be alright
Alright
Alright
Today
On this hot summer day
And the kids are out to play
As I relax, mediate and lay
Everything and everyone
Beautiful in every way

MY GIFT

I think your name is wisdom
Because your knowledge is so great
Your name is love
Because your heart never displays hate
Or maybe your name is strength
Nothing ever knocks you down
Or could your name be faith
With trials and tribulations
God will always be around
Some may say that your name is stubborn
And that may even be true
Maybe it's just another element
That you use to get you through
Your name could be teacher
As the years go on, I continue to learn
One of the greatest lessons
Is that real rewards are not given
They must be earned
Your name is eternity
You could never be erased
Your name is serenity
Because you could never be replaced
The most treasured of them all
That is only mine to claim
My Father
My Gift
That is the very best name

COMMUNICATE

I am judged
Judged because I am
Who I am
Who I want to be
Judged because
I give my love freely
Many feel a lot of things about my existence
Or who I should be
All I do is communicate
I speak love to those who need love
Those who appreciate love
Those who think they can deceive love
And those who don't believe in love
I communicate
My heart does not discriminate
My heart does not allow hate
Should I feel sorry?
Because I communicate to everyone
See I understand hurt
Hurt and I have conversations from time to time
I understand pain
Who whispers while I am asleep
I've even spoken sorrow
The language of self pity
I hear screams of anger from day to day
And because I can't lash out

So I am freed by crying

Letting my tears communicate

To myself

Healing the bruises and scars

I don't need you to give me money

I don't need anyone to make me famous

All I need is to communicate

And for you, yourself, your soul to communicate back to me

I know there are some who understand me

I know there are many who do not

Love is a language that we all know

Have you forgot?

There is not enough people communicating with love

And that is what makes us united

Precious is life

Gifted is knowledge

And strong is peace

Love , I am speaking

Communicating

But I too am getting weak

Not knowing when I can't communicate any longer

So now I must

Communicate stronger

For now

I will communicate love

When I am gone

My spirit will continue to communicate

So please listen

Don't pretend you don't understand
Don't turn away and not listen
Don't judge those
Who do choose to love freely
Like me
I love you

THE OTHER HALF OF MY HEART

Love me

Today, Tomorrow, Forever

You and I together

Many say that if it was meant to be

It will come back again

I threw you away

Not because I did not love you

It was because I was scared

I told myself I wouldn't let anyone hurt me again

And I ended up hurting even more

You took a half of my heart

You kept it warm

You kept it safe

Are you here to give it back to me

Or are you here to let me take the other half of yours

I don't want to play games

That bullshit is for lames

And I can't throw you away

Because you may not come back

Or even worse

I may take my half back

Your touch is like the sweetest candy

I often get angry

Because I thought you were selfish

In not giving me my half

I often think

Why

When there are so many others who will give you their
hearts totally

You have half of mine

Love me

I want you to keep it

Keep it safe

Keep it warm

And wherever you

Or I may go

There is something that you will always know

That you have to love me

Because you have the other half of my heart

THE ABUSE OF A GOOD HEART

Did you know that a good heart is not to be
Abused, refused, misused!
Not to be given the blues
And not to be confused with those
That are bad
Those that make you sad, mad
And made you wish that you
Never had
A heart
To feel
Making you ill
Losing your will
Feeling like you want to kill
Cause they don't understand
A good heart should
Be worth great value
More than any amount that you think should come to you
Any jewels that bling, bling all year through
Worth higher than any stocks, bonds and annuities too.
The greatest investment
This is true
If you had one
Or was in the presence of one
What would you do?
Do you?
How dare you step on the heart that is nothing but good

Did everything and anything that it could

And yet a good heart

Many times goes unnoticed,

Torn apart

Thrown away

And when that happens

It rarely comes back another day

Open your eyes and you will realize

That

A good heart is not to be

Used, abused or confused

With the ones you are used to

If you had one or one was in your presence

Would you know what to do

Do you?

THE GIRL I SAW

The girl I saw

Had beauty beyond compare

And as I continue to stare

She had style that was all her own

But she felt all alone

Because she did not see

What others saw

Like me

I just noticed her today

I knew she saw me before in every way

She never mentioned how she always

Tried to catch my attention

I was too busy to acknowledge her

To even smile at her

To even glance her direction

All she wanted was affection

I see that now

When I look at her

Her smile brings happiness to my day

Her laugh is just to much to say

I wonder if she knows

How beautiful she is

How If possible I wish I could have her kids

She doesn't even think that she is all that

Why?

She thinks she's ugly and fat

And that no one would see

Her heart is like platinum jewelry

I want to apologize

Because I didn't recognize her looking at me

Each and every day

I want to be her friend

Now until the end

I promise before I go

I will let her know

How beautiful she is

I am lucky to be in her presence

I just realized that I love her so

I will be sure to let her know

Because I never want her to leave

Me EVER!!

I will protect her

And tell her how

Others feel the same

As I do

Well not quite

Cause no one loves her more than I do

No one needs her true love

Like me

As I began to talk

As I saw her walk

Towards me

Her smile stopped me in mid verse

I didn't have a speech rehearsed

But I know she knew
What I was going to say
Today
At that moment in time
I was amazed to find
That the girl I saw
That beauty and love so raw
Like Me
Was ME

TO BREATHE

Like a cold winter breeze
Brushing across my face
Like feeling at ease
Everything in its place
Oh how I wish to inhale
With strength so mighty and bold
I would be in a fairytale
Like a warm embrace to hold
Like the sun shining bright
Ocean waters singing in harmony
The visions of a flock of doves in flight
A beautiful sight for all to see
Just take it all in
With no wheezing
Or pain
A blessing coming from within
Oh how I wish to breathe again

GOD SPENT A LITTLE MORE TIME WITH ME

God spent a little time with me
When I was created
He took his time to shape and mold me
In the heavens that are gated
He gave me certain gifts that others do not posses
I know that I am truly blessed
Not saying that
I'm better than all the rest
I know I just pass each and every test
Because he wants me to use and be the best
He gave me a heart of gold
He gave me amazing inner beauty that cannot be sold
He taught me how to continuously give love and not be cold
He showed me how to carry a heavy load
There's one thing for certain that I know for sure
He gave me a soul so rich and pure
Including my own, there is not a broken heart that I can't cure
And there is no pain that I can't endure
The "Golden Rule" is the guide in my life
Through all the hardship and strife
Many look far and near to try to obtain
Many know where it is
But fall by the wayside
Trying to sustain
The key is

You just have to be patient
And try not to complain
There is so much in life and love to gain
When the road has ended
I shall no longer be
I will smile and say
Thank you, Lord
For spending a little more time with me

THE LOVE I HAD FOR YOU I GAVE TO MYSELF YESTERDAY

Why are you coming my way?
I have nothing I want to say
You made your bed and in it you will lay
I suggest you get on your knees and pray
Because
The love I had for you, I gave to myself yesterday
I know you feel bad
Cause you know you lost the best thing you ever had
If it makes you feel better
I am not even mad or sad
As a matter of fact, I am glad
And I'm writing it down on this pad
Why didn't you take heed
You had everything you want and need
You are the one who did not want to proceed
I know I do not need you to succeed
In fact it is all about me indeed
So you are on your own
You can leave me alone
Don't call me on the phone
We both can get out of this horrible comfort zone
So I wish you well
As you go on day by day
Now I know I can't fail
Cause the love I had for you, I gave to myself yesterday

MY HOUSE

The door is open
The stove is on with the smells of home sweet home
A place to rest your head
Sleep and ease your mind, my friend
Come on in
And it's about time for spring cleaning
Shaking out the welcome mat
Always greeting with warm hospitality
Burn the sage
Just in case the evil spirits may have slipped in
They usually stay away
Or if they visit once
They leave quickly never to return
Some try to disguise themselves to see how immaculate it is
And they try to destroy it
Make it dusty and unsanitary
I turn the fire up on the stove just a little
And just smile
They come in
And they eat
They leave angry
At themselves
No longer evil
They see love
It's so bright
Some stop and look into the window

They stare and look for hours, days , months , years

Wondering the door is open

Come on in

Have a seat

AS THE WORLD TURNS

If the world that proceeds you is nothing but darkness
Then the world that is existing is nothing but gloom
Maybe you should wipe your eyes and readjust your sharpness
Not setting yourself up for doom
If the world that proceeds you is nothing but anger
Deceit, lies betrayal and pain
And everywhere you go
You must face danger
You know there is nothing to gain
What's the use
Why not give up
If that is what you see
Because the ultimate excuse
For accepting what does not in fact have to be
Just turning the hands of time
And establishing what is your true need
Not overlooking and disguising the sign
Change the world that is existing
You can most definitely change the world that proceeds
By allowing the light to outshine the darkness
The joy to outshine the pain
The love to consume the hate
And you have everything to gain
Life is a book
And each page you read as you learn
If you take and approach it with a different look

Everything you truly seek will be earned
So if you see the world that proceeds you
And it is not what you would have go your way
The secret on what you must do
Is change the world that is existing today

MY PLEA

Take my body and pump it up with your meds
Saying it will help me live longer
At what cost
That my family has to constantly see me suffer
My limitations on living gets smaller and smaller
My son
Being without a mom
Sometimes my body gets tired
It does not want to fight
It kind of gets angry
I know it gets real angry
With me because I do mistreat it
Not on purpose
But with the notion of trying to make it stronger
Immune to a lot of toxins
It has been violated
 So many times
In so many different ways
It's really tired
It wants to rest
I plead that it will allow me to exist on this earth
I promise to protect it to the best of my ability
I will leave it in God's hands
I know if my body lays to rest
My soul will not
It will always stay strong

And never feel violated
My love will continue to provide what is has been doing
Since my existence
My body is only temporary
As with all of us here
Right now I plea with my body
Not to yet expire
I have many tasks to accomplish
Many dreams to make a reality
My son to graduate from college
And see me to be the best
As best will have me to be

DAYDREAM

As you look across the sky
And see what the outside has in store each and every day
As the wind blows and birds fly high
Each tree so perfect
Placed in a unique way
As the planes soar
And the sun beams bake our skin
As the water waves brush the shore
Over and over again
You close your eyes and hear the sounds of the land
The sounds of the mountains and seas
The sounds of man
Smell the fresh air
The flowers
Home cooked meals
Aromas from everywhere
And on every city
On every street
In every housed
There is a story
Each a page in the book
The book called life
And what comes to mind
As the pages turn
How blessed we truly are

REBECCA AND ME

Rebecca and me
We
Together made history
Rebecca the nurturer
The teacher
The provider
Her smile spoke in words
Unspeakable
Her grace glided across
Unstoppable
Her beauty breathtaking
With me a small child listening
Feeling the warmth
That constant positivity
That Rebecca had
Man, you would have never wanted her to leave your presence
She always made sure that everything is okay
And when she called you. "Love"
You my friend were special
I was "boobie"
From the beginning and will always remain the same for eternity
Rebecca
As the years went by to hear her voice would put my heart at ease
Rebecca and me
Together
She will always be my angel

She has left to prepare
The other side for me
Up in the heavens above
Shining brightly
She still lets me know everything is okay
I miss her dearly
And I know she sees
But she served her purpose
And now it's time for her to be at peace
But Rebecca and me will always be
Together
For Eternity
I love you, Aunt Jean

HEY MY FRIEND-COLLEGE GRADUATION DAY

Hey My friend

Being that today is a big day for me

Being that today is another step to my destiny

Being today is not just an ordinary day

To you my friend there is something I must say

Along this journey I've discovered treasures, fortunes
and misfortunes

Which now I know

They were all a part of life

And along the way I realized that the path I walked on through-
out the years was not the path that was chosen for me

Yet it was the path I chose

The people who I had to fight

The people who I most feared and despised

The people whom I saw as my friends and later became enemies

The ones who were enemies all along were a reflection of me

Because I gave a part of myself

My energy

My livelihood

Why

For acceptance

For happiness

For love

All along the one true person who I fought the hardest and
despised the most and was the worst enemy

Who I only gave part of myself and my energy to

I completely did not acknowledge this person was even there asking me

For acceptance

For happiness

For love

And it was through these reflections of these people

That I saw that person who I hated so much was me

How could I expect from others that I could not give to myself, first

If I did it that way maybe my path wouldn't have been so bumpy

So, trying and so painful in many ways

I became aware that knowledge will never lead you on the wrong path

It will always guide you in the right direction

I say this to you my friend because

I want to be the reflection of you

Instead of me fighting negative, I will now face it with the positive

It's not worth fighting yourself because

People may come and go

In and out of your life

But you have to deal with you as long as you are on this earth

As long as your heart beat

My friend I'm speaking the truth

When I say that knowledge will allow you to get acceptance

The happiness, The love

Knowledge

Knowing who you are and the path you have chosen and why
Opening your eyes, heart and ears
Knowing your reflections
It is not about just beauty or how much money
Being the wealthiest person is having true knowledge of yourself
It's not about who 's physically strongest
Who can answer a question faster
Intelligence, my friend is knowing the path that you are walking
Know your environment
Know your surroundings
Know not to be the enemy
Listen
I am a reflection of you
Hey my friend,
Find the reflection of yourself.

ABOUT THE AUTHOR

Betrice Coleman-Sweet started writing at an early age about her life experiences growing up in South Central Los Angeles. It started out with poetry and short stories. She gave birth to her son, RaShaun in 1992 at 16 years old. She was a high achiever throughout her school years including college.

In 2004, Betrice met her life partner, Bea Sweet. They later tied the knot in Big Bear California in May of 2005.

In 2010, she began writing articles and blogs. Throughout her career, she was asked to edit and write key documents for notable corporations and non-profit organizations. Some of her articles and blogs have been published on various renowned media outlets such as Yahoo, LA Times, Variety and News-Press.

B's love for communication and community compelled her to create Serving Angels Media in February 2009. Her vision is to uplift and "shine the light" on the individuals, organizations, and companies whose purpose is to give to the communities in which they serve. Serving Angels, a "full-service" Communications Consulting Firm. Betrice is a communications coach with an emphasis on storytelling through strategic planning, social marketing, blogging, public relations, event coordination, and executive coaching. Serving Angels Media also hosted workshops presented by transformational, leadership, and community leaders throughout Los Angeles. She is diligent with assessing her client's needs and support them with getting their message out into the world.. Her past clients include celebrities, public figures, several prominent businesses and non-profit organizations. The motto for Serving Angels is "Serving The People Who Serve".

In summer 2012, B became a graduate of Americorp's Public Allies Los Angeles Program which allowed her to serve the community and strengthen her leadership development skills. Public Allies is also where she was voted by her peers and staff as "The Hugganista" because she loves to give big hugs.

Betrice is currently the General Manager at Black Onyx World, LLC in Fort Myers, Florida. She has been with the company for over 6 years.

Her resounding passion involves empowering people to own their stories as a way to connect and ignite social change one community at a time.

Betrice is a mother, wife, writer, community server, and evolutionary hugger.